Lena Eckhoff

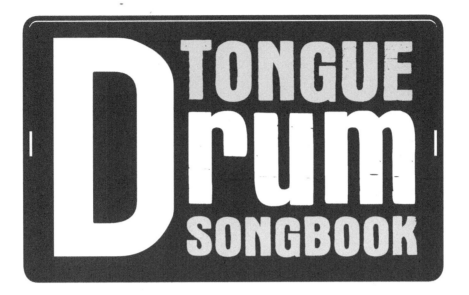

Merry Christmas!

Christmas Songs
for diatonic tongue drum
(8 - 11 - 13 tongue models)

Lena Eckhoff
Tongue Drum Songbook, Merry Christmas!
All rights reserved.
le.eckhoff@gmail.com

© 2021

Revised edition 2023

ISBN: 9798730699151

Preface

Hello fellow players,

and welcome to this collection of popular Christmas songs. I've selected songs that are easy to play and sound great on your tongue drum. And although I had to omit a few Christmas songs because they can't be played on a TD, there still are more than enough left you'll love to play.

This book is written for the beginning player. All songs are arranged for easy tongue drum (8, 11 and 13 tongue diatonic models in C*).

To make playing as easy as possible I'm using large notation and an extra line of tongue drum tablature—reading music not required! (more on TD tablature on p. 14)

For those interested in learning to read music, there's an introduction to the most important basics at the end of the book.

Wishing you a merry tongue drum Christmas,

Lena Eckhoff

* The songs in this book can not be played on **pentatonic** tongue drums (TD models missing the numbers 4 and 7).

While this book was written for 8 and 11 tongue models primarily, some songs contain notes that can only be played on 13 tongue models. With a little bit of imagination you can replace these with notes available on 8 and 11 tongue models, though.

Contents

Playing tongue drum

Songs

Your tongue drum

Your tongue drum (tong drum, tank drum or hap drum) is a member of the percussion instruments family. It is constructed from two steel "bowls", joined and sealed at the edges with a sound hole at the bottom of the instrument and several steel "tongues" (usually 8-13) radially cut from the top.
Tongue drums originally were hand-cut and welded from used propane cylinders, but today are made of precision-machined steel. Some models feature magnetic sliding weights at the underside of the tongues for easy tuning.
They have a bell-like tone most people tend to like at once.

Your tongue drum has a close relative, the handpan* (hank drum, UFO drum or zen drum). Handpans are significantly bigger, most don't have tongues and they look a lot like "inverted" steel drums (even the name handpan is often seen as short for steelpan played by hand). Their manufacturing process is far more complicated and as a result they're more expensive than tongue drums.

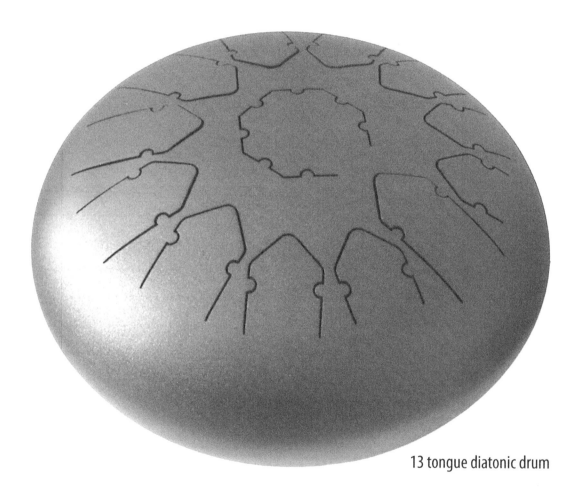

13 tongue diatonic drum

* The original instrument and eponym of the handpan family was designed by Felix Rohner and Sabina Schaerer based on ancient percussion instruments like gong, gamelan and bells.

ongue drum care and tuning

Your tongue drum doesn't need much in the care department. Use the bag or case it came in to store it when not playing and clean its surface from time to time with a soft cloth.

Your tongue drum is factory-tuned. This is a "tuning for life" so you don't have to regularly tune your drum like you would a violin or a guitar (there are professional tunable instruments, but that's another story).

If, however, one or more tongues of your drum are out of tune you can correct their tuning by sticking a small neodym magnet to the back of the tongue. Experiment with the magnet's position and use a chromatic tuner (or a smartphone app) to check for correct tuning.

chromatic tuner

I do not recommend tuning methods like bending the tongues or even filing them—tuning this way can irreparably damage your drum and should best be left to professionals.

Some drums are shipped with a piece of plastic sealing the sound hole. For the best sound remove it prior to playing.

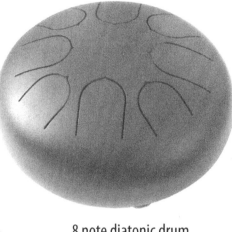

8 note diatonic drum

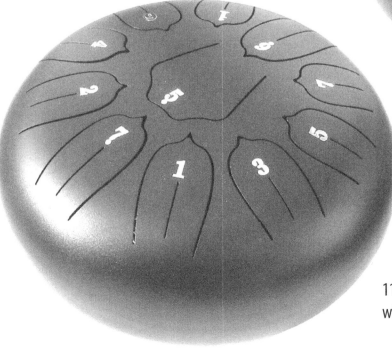

11 note diatonic drum
with stickers

You can position your tongue drum in your lap or on any flat surface like a table top (many tongue drums have small rubber seals at their bottom side for just this purpose). You can also use a snare drum stand. This is especially handy when you want to play standing up.

Always take care not to block the resonance hole at the instruments' bottom, though.

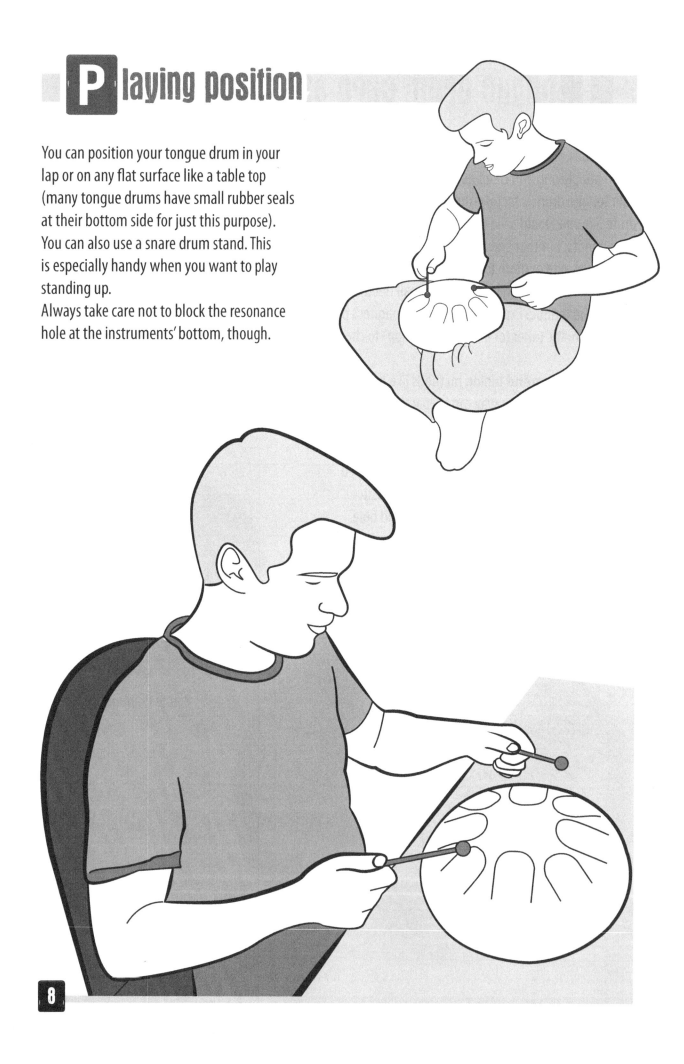

There are basically three ways to play your tongue drum:

1. Playing with mallets

Playing with mallets is the easiest way to produce a loud and clear tone with a distinctive pitch. Most tongue drums come with two mallets, one for each hand. If your drum didn't include mallets, you can buy them at your local music store or on the internet. If you're a beginning player, I'd suggest playing with mallets until you've developed a basic feel for the instrument. Once you've achieved this, experiment with all playing techniques and see what feels best to you. You can even combine all three techniques for a whole world of exciting sounds!

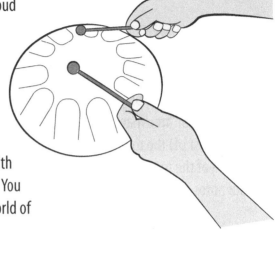

2. Playing with fingerpicks

These are worn on your finger(s) with the little rubber bulge pointing downward. Just as playing with your fingers, producing a clear tone takes a bit of practice.

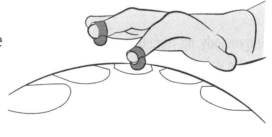

3. Playing with your fingers

This is the most basic and intuitive method to play tongue drum, offering lots of tonal possibilities and sound effects. There's a downside to it, though: it takes a little bit of practice to produce a clear tone.

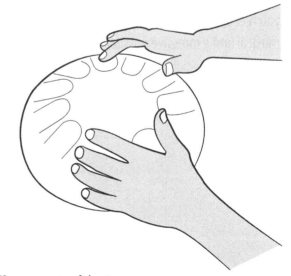

 You can create different sounds by hitting different parts of the tongue, with the fullest sound produced near the tip.

Damping

Another important playing technique is called damping. This simply means stopping the vibration (and hence the sound) of one or more tongues.
There are basically two different ways of damping.

1. You may want to keep the tongues you're not playing from ringing along to the ones you are playing. To do this, rest your "free" hand lightly on all (or most of) the tongues you're not playing at the moment. This will give your notes a very clean sound.

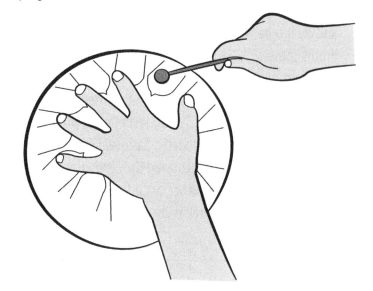

2. When playing melody, it's sometimes best to damp the notes shortly after you've played them. This can be done with your "free" hand or with the side of your playing hand. Lightly touch the tongue to stop its vibration.

Try both of these techniques to develop a general feel for the sound produced and use them whenever you feel appropriate. I believe you'll soon discover that damping can be a very nice addition to your musical and expressive possibilities.

The notes on your tongue drum

There are literally dozens of different types of tongue drums which differ mainly due to their note layout (the notes you can play on them). Here are some of the more common tongue drum note layouts so you can check and find out what type of drum you're playing. Most tongue drums sold today have tongue **numbers printed on or bonded** to their tongues, so checking this should be easy.

8 note (pentatonic) 5̣ 6̣ 1 2 3 5 6 i̇

This drum is missing some of the scale notes you'll need for many songs: scale notes 4 and 7. This type of drum (**pentatonic**) is better suited for meditation and improvising than for playing songs.
(This drum is mentioned here just for the sake of completeness).

8 note (diatonic) 1 2 3 4 5 6 7 i̇

This type of drum contains all the notes of the major scale, meaning there's quite a lot of songs you can play on this drum.

11 note (diatonic) 5̣ 6̣ 7̣ 1 2 3 4 5 6 7 i̇

This is basically an 8 note tongue drum with three additional bass notes (you won't need these additional notes for the songs in this book, though)

13 note (diatonic) 5̣ 6̣ 7̣ 1 2 3 4 5 6 7 i̇ 2̇ 3̇

This is an 11 note TD with two additional high notes. And while most of the songs in this book can be played on either an 8 note or an 11 note TD model, a select few can only be played on a 13 note TD. I've marked them with this symbol:

Wanting to play 13 note TD songs on an 8 tongue or 11 tongue model? Just use your ear and your imagination to replace missing notes by other good-sounding notes on your TD (try to find notes complementing the songs' melody, though).

Have a look at the next page to see the tongue layout of the different TD types and the corresponding notes (notes not available on a particular model in grey).

8 note
(pentatonic tuning in C)

8 note
(diatonic tuning in C)

Keep in mind that these are just the most common TD layouts. If your TD's layout is different, carefully compare the tongue numbers.

11 note
(diatonic tuning in C)

13 note
(diatonic tuning in C)

 These are the notes for diatonic tongue drums in C. If your drum isn't tuned to C (C is the most common tuning, but G and D are also popular), just play by the TAB numbers. The song(s) will still sound "right", just a little bit lower or higher in pitch.

The tongue drum **can** be notated as any other musical instrument using what is called **standard notation** (notes). In fact, that's what all the songs in this book are notated in and it's fine if you **can** read music. But what about those of us who **can't (or don't want to) read music**?

That's fine, too—just use the extra line of **tongue drum TAB** (short for tablature) written below the standard notation. Using tongue drum TAB you can play without having to read music. In tongue drum TAB the letters exactly correspond to the tongue numbers printed on your drum—it's as easy as that!

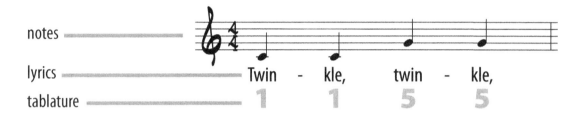

So if you see, for example, the letter "1" below a note, strike tongue 1 with your mallet; for the letter "5", strike tongue 5 etc. This also applies to tongue numbers with a little dot above or below the number: they're written exactly like this in TAB, too.
(Some tongue drums don't have printed numbers, but include self-adhesive stickers you have to fit to your drum yourself. Compare your drum to the graphics on p. 12+13 and fit the stickers accordingly.)

As mentioned in the section on tongue drum layout, not all tongue drums have the same number of notes. Many small tongue drums are missing note numbers 4 and/or 7, so you obviously can't play songs with these numbers in them. This is one of the reasons I recommend getting an 11 tongue model (or even a 13 tongue model): there's just so much more music you can play on the bigger models.

But you can also just improvise on your tongue drum, playing whatever feels right and sounds good to you, of course. This is where the smaller tongue drums can come into their own. Most smaller tongue drums are tuned to just 5 different notes (even if some of them are included more than once). This is called a **pentatonic tuning** (penta = greek = five).

Twinkle, twinkle, little star

Twin - kle, twin - kle, lit - tle star,
1 1 5 5 6 6 5

how I won - der what you are!
4 4 3 3 2 2 1

Up a - bove the world so high, like a dia - mond
5 5 4 4 3 3 2 5 5 4 4

in the sky! Twin - kle, twin - kle, lit - tle star,
3 3 2 1 1 5 5 6 6 5

how I won - der what you are!
4 4 3 3 2 2 1

2. When the blazing sun is gone,
   when he nothing shines upon,
   then you show your little light,
   twinkle, twinkle, all the night.

3. Then the traveller in the dark,
   thanks you for your tiny spark,
   he could not see which way to go,
   if you did not twinkle so.

4. In the dark blue sky you keep,
   and often through my curtains peep,
   for you never shut your eye,
   till the sun is in the sky.

5. As your bright and tiny spark,
   lights the traveller in the dark,
   though I know not what you are,
   twinkle, twinkle, little star.

The first Noel

2. They looked up and saw a star
   shining in the east beyond them far,
   and to the earth it gave great light,
   and so it continued both day and night.

3. And by the light of that same star,
   three wise men came from country far;
   To seek for a king was their intent,
   and to follow the star wherever it went.

4. This star drew nigh to the northwest,
   o'er Bethlehem it took it rest,
   and there it did both stop and stay
   right over the place where Jesus lay.

5. Then entered in those wise men three
   full reverently upon their knee,
   and offered there in his presence
   their gold, and myrrh, and frankincense.

6. Then let us all with one accord
   sing praises to our heavenly Lord;
   That hath made heaven and earth of naught,
   and with his blood mankind hath bought.

Christ was born on Christmas day

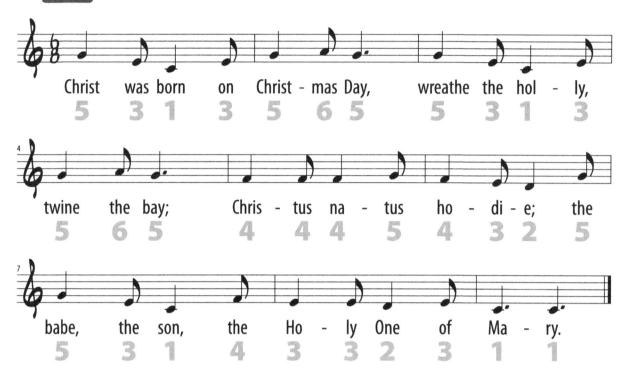

Christ was born on Christ - mas Day,
5   3   1   3   5   6   5
wreathe the hol - ly,
5   3   1   3

twine the bay; Chris - tus na - tus ho - di - e; the
5   6   5   4   4   4   5   4   3   2   5

babe, the son, the Ho - ly One of Ma - ry.
5   3   1   4   3   3   2   3   1   1

2. He is born to set us free,
   He is born our Lord to be,
   ex Maria Virgine,
   the God, the Lord, by all adored forever.

3. Let the bright red berries glow,
   ev'ry where in goodly show,
   Christus natus hodie;
   the Babe, the Son, the Holy One of Mary.

4. Christian men, rejoice and sing,
   tis the birthday of a King
   ex Maria Virgine;
   The God, the Lord, by all adored forever.

5. Sing out with bliss,
   His name is this: Immanuel!
   As 'twas foretold in days of old,
   by Gabriel.

Jesu, joy of man's desiring

Je - su,   joy   of   man's   de - si - ring,   ho - ly
3   4   5   5   4   3   2   2   3   4

wis - dom,   love   most   bright.   Drawn   by
5   3   2 3 4 3   2   1   3   4

Thee,   our   souls   as - pir - ing,   soar   to   un - cre -
5   5   4   3   2   2   3   4   5   3

at - ed   light.   Word   of   God,   our
2 3 4 3   2   1   2   3   4   4

flesh   that   fash - ioned,   with   the   fire   of
3   4 5 3   2   2   4   5   6   6

life   im - pas-sioned,   Striv - ing   still   to   truth un -
5   6 5 5   4   4   3   4   5   5   4   3

known.   soar - ing.   dy - ing   'round   Thy   throne.
2   3   4   5   3   2   3 4 3 2   1

2. Through the way where hope is guiding,
   hark, what peaceful music rings;
   Where the flock, in Thee confiding,
   drink of joy from deathless springs.
   Theirs is beauty's fairest pleasure;
   theirs is wisdom's holiest treasure.
   Thou dost ever lead Thine own,
   In the love of joys unknown.

2. Christ by highest heav'n adored,
   Christ the everlasting Lord!
   Late in time behold Him come,
   offspring of a virgin's womb.
   Veiled in flesh the Godhead see,
   hail the incarnate deity!
   Pleased as man with man to dwell,
   Jesus, our Emmanuel,
   Hark! The herald angels sing,
   "Glory to the newborn king!"

3. Hail the heav'n-born prince of peace,
   hail the son of righteousness!
   Light and life to all He brings,
   Ris'n with healing in His wings.
   Mild He lays His glory by,
   born that man no more may die!
   Born to raise the sons of earth,
   born to give them second birth!
   Hark! The herald angels sing,
   "Glory to the newborn king!"

I saw three ships

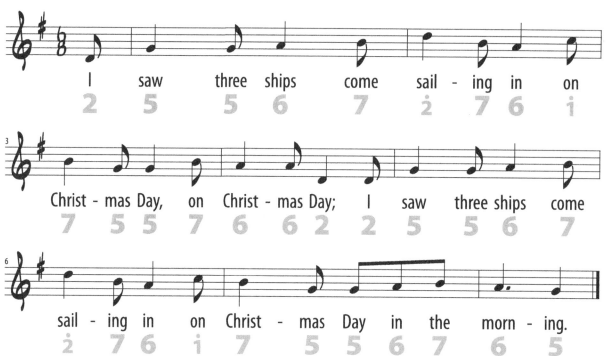

2. And what was in those ships all three,
   on Christmas Day, on Christmas Day?
   And what was in those ships all three,
   on Christmas Day in the morning?

3. The Virgin Mary and Christ were there,
   on Christmas Day, on Christmas Day;
   The Virgin Mary and Christ were there,
   on Christmas Day in the morning.

4. Pray, wither sailed those ships all three,
   on Christmas Day, on Christmas Day;
   Pray, wither sailed those ships all three,
   on Christmas Day in the morning.

5. O they sailed into Bethlehem,
   on Christmas Day, on Christmas Day;
   O they sailed into Bethlehem,
   on Christmas Day in the morning.

6. And all the bells on earth shall ring,
   on Christmas Day, on Christmas Day;
   And all the bells on earth shall ring,
   on Christmas Day in the morning.

7. And all the Angels in Heaven shall sing,
   on Christmas Day, on Christmas Day;
   And all the angels in heaven shall sing,
   on Christmas Day in the morning.

8. And all the souls on earth shall sing,
   on Christmas Day, on Christmas Day;
   And all the souls on earth shall sing,
   on Christmas Day in the morning.

9. Then let us all rejoice again,
   on Christmas Day, on Christmas Day;
   Then let us all rejoice again,
   on Christmas Day in the morning.

While____ shep - herds watched their flocks by___ night all___
3 4 5 i 7 6 5 1 2 3 3 4

seat - ed on the___ ground;___ the___ an - gel of the
5 5 5 4 3 3 2 7 i ż 5 4 4

Lord came___ down and____ glo - ry shone a - round___ and
4 3 2 3 i 7 6 5 4 3 6 5 ż

glo - ry shone a - round.
5 i 3 2 1

2. "Fear not," he said
   for mighty dread,
   had seized their troubled minds;
   "Glad tidings of great joy I bring,
   to you and all mankind,
   to you and all mankind."

3. "To you in David's
   town this day,
   is born of David's line;
   the Savior who is Christ the Lord
   and this shall be the sign,
   and this shall be the sign."

4. "The heavenly Babe,
   you there shall find,
   to human view displayed;
   And meanly wrapped in swathing bands,
   and in a manger laid,
   and in a manger laid."

5. Thus spake the seraph,
   and forthwith,
   appeared a shining throng.
   Of angels praising God, who thus
   addressed their joyful song,
   addressed their joyful song.

6. "All glory be to
   God on high,
   and to the earth be peace;
   Goodwill henceforth
   from heaven to men,
   begin and never cease
   begin and never cease!"

Angels we have heard on high

An - gels we have heard on high sweet - ly sing - ing
7 7 7 2 2 i 7 7 6 7 2

o'er the plains. And the moun - tains in re-ply,
7 6 5 7 7 7 2 2 i 7

ech - o - ing their joy - ous strains. Glo - - - -
7 6 7 2 7 6 5 2 3 2 i 7

- - - - - - - - - - - ri - a
i 2 i 7 6 7 i 7 6 5 6 2 2

in ex - cel - sis De - o, Glo - - - -
5 6 7 i 7 6 2 3 2 i 7

- - - - - - - - - - - ri - a
i 2 i 7 6 7 i 7 6 5 6 2 2

in ex - cel - sis De - - - o.
5 6 7 i 7 6 5

2. Shepherds, why this jubilee?
   Why your joyous strains prolong?
   What the gladsome tidings be
   which inspire your heavenly song?

3. Come to Bethlehem and see,
   Him whose birth the angels sing;
   Come, adore on bended knee
   Christ, the Lord, the newborn King!

4. See Him in a manger laid,
   Jesus, Lord of heaven and earth!
   Mary, Joseph, lend your aid,
   with us sing our Savior's birth.

2. Still through the cloven skies they come,
   with peaceful wings unfurled;
   And still their heavenly music floats,
   o'er all the weary world.
   Above its sad and lowly plains,
   they bend on hovering wing.
   And ever o'er its Babel sounds
   The blessed angels sing.

3. O ye beneath life's crushing load,
   whose forms are bending low;
   Who toil along the climbing way
   with painful steps and slow.
   Look now, for glad and golden hours
   come swiftly on the wing.
   Oh rest beside the weary road,
   and hear the angels sing.

4. For lo! the days are hastening on,
   by prophets seen of old;
   When with the ever-circling years,
   shall come the time foretold.
   When the new heaven and earth shall own,
   the prince of peace, their king.
   And the whole world send back the song,
   which now the angels sing.

Deck the halls

2. See the blazing Yule before us,
   fa-la-la-la-la, la-la-la-la,
   strike the lamp and join the chorus,
   fa-la-la-la-la, la-la-la-la.
   Follow me in merry measure,
   fa-la-la-la-la, la-la-la-la,
   while I tell of yuletide treasure,
   fa-la-la-la-la, la-la-la-la.

3. Fast away the old year passes,
   fa-la-la-la-la, la-la-la-la,
   hail the new year, ye lads and lasses,
   fa-la-la-la-la, la-la-la-la.
   Sing we joyous all together,
   fa-la-la-la-la, la-la-la-la,
   heedless of the wind and weather,
   fa-la-la-la-la, la-la-la-la.

Over the river and through the woods

2. Over the river and through the woods,
   to have a first-rate play;
   Oh, hear the bells ring, „Ting-a-ling-ling!"
   Hurrah for Thanksgiving Day!
   Over the river and through the woods,
   trot fast, my dapple gray!
   Spring over the ground like a hunting hound!
   For this is Thanksgiving day.

3. Over the river and through the woods,
   and straight through the barnyard gate.
   We seem to go extremely slow
   it is so hard to wait!
   Over the river and through the woods,
   now Grandmother's cap I spy!
   Hurrah for the fun! Is the pudding done?
   Hurrah for the pumpkin pie!

Go, tell it on the mountain

Go, tell it on the moun-tain   o-ver   the hills   and
7   7 6 5 3 2   5   6 6   5 6   5 6

ev' - ry - where.   Go,   tell   it on   the moun - tain that
7 5 3 2   7   7 6 5 3 2   5 i

Je-sus Christ is born. When I was a see-ker I
7 7   6   6   5   2 6   5 6   7 5   2

sought both night and day.   I asked the Lord to
6   6 5   6   7 i   2 6   6 5   6

help me   and He showed me the way.
7 5   i 7 5 6 6 5

2. He made me a watchman upon the city wall,
   and if I am a Christian I am the least of all.

3. 'T was a lowly manger that Jesus Christ was born,
   the Lord sent down an angel that bright and glorious morn'.

Joy to the world

2. Joy to the world, the savior reigns.
   Let men their songs employ.
   While fields and floods, rocks, hills, and plains,
   repeat the sounding joy,
   repeat the sounding joy,
   repeat, repeat the sounding joy.

3. No more let sin and sorrows grow,
   nor thorns infest the ground,
   He comes to make His blessings flow,
   far as the curse is found,
   far as the curse is found,
   far as, far as the curse is found.

4. He rules the world with truth and grace,
   and makes the nations prove,
   the glories of His righteousness,
   and wonders of His love,
   and wonders of His love,
   and wonders, wonders of His love.

Away in a manger

A - way in a man - ger, no crib for His
2 2 1 7 7 6 5 5 5 3

bed, the litt - le Lord Je - sus laid down His sweet
2 2 2 3 2 2 6 6 3 2 5

head. The stars in the bright sky looked down where He
7 2 2 1 7 7 6 5 5 5 3

lay, the lit - tle Lord Je - sus, a - sleep on the hay.
2 2 1 7 6 7 6 5 6 3 6 5

2. The cattle are lowing
   the poor baby wakes.
   But little Lord Jesus
   no crying He makes.
   I love Thee, Lord Jesus,
   look down from the sky
   and stay by my side,
   'til morning is nigh.

3. Be near me, Lord Jesus,
   I ask Thee to stay.
   Close by me forever
   and love me I pray.
   Bless all the dear children
   in Thy tender care
   and take us to heaven
   to live with Thee there.

Chorus
He is born, the holy child,
play the oboe and bagpipes merrily!
He is born, the holy child,
sing we all of the Savior mild.

2. O how lovely, O how pure,
   is this perfect child of heaven;
   O how lovely, O how pure,
   gracious gift of God to man!
   He is born, the holy child . . .

3. Jesus, Lord of all the world,
   coming as a child among us,
   Jesus, Lord of all the world,
   grant to us Thy heavenly peace.
   He is born, the holy child . . .

2. Our God, heaven cannot hold him,
   nor earth sustain;
   Heaven and earth shall flee away,
   when He comes to reign.
   In the bleak midwinter,
   a stable place sufficed,
   the Lord God incarnate,
   Jesus Christ.

3. Enough for him, whom Cherubim,
   worship night and day;
   A breast full of milk,
   and a manger full of hay.
   Enough for him, whom angels,
   fall down before,
   the ox and ass and camel,
   which adore.

4. Angels and archangels,
   may have gathered there;
   Cherubim and seraphim,
   thronged the air.
   But his mother only,
   in her maiden bliss,
   worshipped the beloved,
   with a kiss.

5. What can I give him,
   poor as I am?
   If I were a shepherd,
   I would bring a lamb.
   If I were a wise man,
   I would do my part,
   yet what I can I give Him —
   give my heart.

Jol - ly old Saint Nich - o - las,   lean your ear this   way.
6   6   6   6   5   5   5   4   4   4   4   6

Don't you tell a   sin - gle soul   what I'm going to   say.
2   2   2   2   1   1   4   5   4   5   6   5

Christ-mas Eve is   com - ing soon.   Now, you dear old   man,
6   6   6   6   5   5   5   4   4   4   4   6

whis - per what you'll   bring to me;   tell me if you   can.
2   2   2   2   1   1   4   5   4   5   6   4

2. When the clock is striking twelve,
   when I'm fast asleep,
   down the chimney broad and black,
   with your pack you'll creep;
   All the stockings you will find
   hanging in a row;
   Mine will be the shortest one,
   you'll be sure to know.

3. Johnny wants a pair of skates;
   Susy wants a dolly;
   Nellie wants a story book;
   She thinks dolls are folly;
   As for me, my little brain
   isn't very bright;
   Choose for me, old Santa Claus,
   what you think is right.

Still, still, still

Still, still, still, the night is cold and chill! The
7 6 5 2 7 7 6 6 5 2

vir - gin's ten - der arms en - fol - ding, warm and safe the
1 1 6 6 2 2 7 7 1 1 6 6

Christ child hold-ing. Still, still, still, the night is cold and chill.
2 2 7 7 7 6 5 2 7 7 6 6 5

2. Dream, dream, dream,
   He sleeps, the Savior King.
   While guardian angels watch beside Him,
   Mary tenderly will guide Him.
   Dream, dream, dream,
   He sleeps, the Savior King.

O come, little children

O, come, lit-tle child-ren, o, come, one and all, to
5 5 3 5 5 3 5 4 2 4 3 5

Beth - le-hem's stab - le, in Beth - le - hem's stall. And
5 3 5 5 3 5 4 2 4 3 3

see with re - joic - ing this glo - ri - ous sight, our
2 2 2 4 4 4 3 3 3 6 6

Fath - er in hea - ven has sent us this night.
5 5 5 i 5 3 5 4 2 1

Up on the house - top___ rein - deer pause,
5 5 6 5 3 2 1 3 5

out jumps good old San - ta Claus. Down through the chim - ney with
6 6 5 3 2 5 5 5 5 6 5 3 2

lots of toys, all for the lit - tle ones'
1 3 5 6 6 6 5 5 3

Christ - mas joys. Ho, ho, ho! Who would-n't go!
2 5 1 4 4 6 5 5 5 3

Ho, ho, ho! Who would-n't go! Up on the house - top,
2 4 4 3 5 5 1 5 5 6 5 3

click, click, click. Down through the chim - ney with good Saint Nick.
4 5 6 5 5 6 5 3 3 2 5 1

The boar's head carol

The boar's head in hand bear I, be-deck'd with bays and
5 i i i 7 i 5 3 4 4 6 4

rose - mar-y; and I pray you, my mas - ters, be mer - ry, quot
5 5 i 5 5 i i i i 7 i 5 3

es - tis in con - vi - vi - o. Ca - put ap - ri
4 4 6 4 5 5 i i i 7 7

de - fe - ro red - dens lau - des Do - mi - no.
i i 5 4 4 6 4 5 5 i

Quot estis in convivio = As many as are in the feast
Caput apri defero = The boar's head I bear
Reddens laudes Domino = Giving praise to the Lord

2. The boar's head, as I understand,
   is the rarest dish in all this land,
   which thus bedeck'd with a gay garland,
   let us servire cantico.
   Caput apri defero,
   reddens laudes Domino.

3. Our steward hath provided this
   in honour of the King of Bliss,
   which on this day to be served is,
   in reginensi atrio.
   Caput apri defero,
   reddens laudes Domino.

O Sanctissima

O thou hap - - py, O thou ho - - ly,
5 6 5 4 3 4 5 6 5 4 3 4

glo - rious peace bring-ing Christ-mas time! An - gel throngs to
5 5 6 7 i 7 6 5 2 3 2 3

meet Thee, on Thy birth we greet____ Thee:
4 5 4 3 4 3 4 5 6 5

Hail to Christ, the Son of God, our new - born king!
i 7 6 5 i 6 5 4 3 2 1

Here we come a-was-sail-ing a-mong the leaves so
1 2 3 2 1 2 3 2 1 5 5 5

green. Here we come a-wan-d'ring so fair to be
5 6 6 5 3 5 4 3 2 1 2 3

seen. Love and joy come to you, and to
4 3 4 5 i 6 5 3 4

you your was-sail too. And God bless you and
5 5 i 6 5 3 4 5 6 3

send you a Hap - py New Year and God
4 2 1 2 1 2 3 1 4 3 4

send you a Hap - py New Year.
5 6 3 4 2 1 2 1

2. Our wassail cup is made
   of the rosemary tree,
   and so is your beer
   of the best barley.
   Love and joy come to you ...

3. We are not daily beggars
   that beg from door to door;
   But we are neighbours' children,
   whom you have seen before.
   Love and joy come to you ...

4. Call up the butler of this house,
   put on his golden ring.
   Let him bring us up a glass of beer,
   and better we shall sing.
   Love and joy come to you ...

5. We have got a little purse
   of stretching leather skin;
   We want a little of your money
   to line it well within.
   Love and joy come to you ...

6. Bring us out a table
   and spread it with a cloth;
   Bring us out a mouldy cheese,
   and some of your Christmas loaf.
   Love and joy come to you ...

7. God bless the master of this house
   likewise the mistress too,
   and all the little children
   that round the table go.
   Love and joy come to you ...

O holy night

O Hol - y Night,____ the stars are bright - ly shin -
3 3   3   5   5   6   6   4   6 i

ing. It is the night of the dear Sav - iour's birth.____
5   5 3   2   4   3   4   5   4   2   1

Long lay the world____ in sin and er - ror pin -
3   3   3   5   5   6   6   4   6 i

ing, till He ap - peared and the soul felt its worth.____ A
5   5   5   3   7   5   6   7   i   7   3   5

thrill of hope the wea - ry world re - joic - es, for
5   6   2   5   6   5   i   3   6   5   5

yon - der breaks a new and glo - rious morn.
5   6   2   5   6   5   i   3   5

Fall_____ on your knees!____ O, hear
i   7   6   7   7   2

2. Led by the light of faith serenely beaming,
   with glowing hearts by His cradle we stand.
   O'er the world a star is sweetly gleaming,
   now come the wisemen from out of the Orient land.
   The King of kings lay thus lowly manger;
   In all our trials born to be our friends.
   He knows our need, our weakness is no stranger,
   behold your King! Before him lowly bend!

3. Truly He taught us to love one another,
   His law is love and His gospel is peace.
   Chains he shall break, for the slave is our brother.
   And in his name all oppression shall cease.
   Sweet hymns of joy in grateful chorus raise we,
   with all our hearts we praise His holy name.
   Christ is the Lord! Then ever, ever praise we,
   His power and glory ever more proclaim!

Wassail, wassail

Was - sail! was - sail!___ all o - ver the
2   5   5   5   6   7   i   7   6

town,___ our toast it is white and our
7   ż   ż   i   6   6   6   7   i

ale___ it___ is brown. Our bowl___ it___ is___
7 6 5 6 7   6   i   7 6 5 6 7 i

made of the white ma - ple tree; with the
ż   ż i 7 5 7   6   5 2

was - saili - ng bowl, we'll drink___ to thee.
7   6 7 i   7 6 5 6 5

2. Here's to our horse, and to his right ear,
   God send our master a happy new year:
   A happy new year as e'er he did see,
   with my wassailing bowl I drink to thee.

3. So here is to Cherry and to his right cheek
   pray God send our master a good piece of beef
   and a good piece of beef that may we all see
   with the wassailing bowl, we'll drink to thee.

4. Here's to our mare, and to her right eye,
   God send our mistress a good Christmas pie;
   A good Christmas pie as e'er I did see,
   with my wassailing bowl I drink to thee.

5. So here is to Broad Mary and to her broad horn,
   may God send our master a good crop of corn,
   and a good crop of corn that may we all see,
   with the wassailing bowl, we'll drink to thee.

6. And here is to Fillpail and to her left ear,
   pray God send our master a happy New Year,
   and a happy New Year as e'er he did see,
   with the wassailing bowl, we'll drink to thee.

7. Here's to our cow, and to her long tail,
   God send our master us never may fail
   of a cup of good beer: I pray you draw near,
   and our jolly wassail it's then you shall hear.

8. Come butler, come fill us a bowl of the best,
   then we hope that your soul in heaven may rest,
   but if you do draw us a bowl of the small,
   then down shall go butler, bowl and all.

9. Be here any maids? I suppose here be some;
   Sure they will not let young men stand on the cold stone!
   Sing hey O, maids! come trole back the pin,
   and the fairest maid in the house let us all in.

10. Then here's to the maid in the lily white smock,
    who tripped to the door and slipped back the lock,
    who tripped to the door and pulled back the pin,
    for to let these jolly wassailers in.

While by my sheep

3. There shall the child lie in a stall,
   this child who shall redeem us all.
   How great our joy ...

4. This gift of God we'll cherish well,
   that ever joy our hearts shall fill.
   How great our joy ...

How to read music

On the following pages we've compiled the most important basics of music notation. Don't worry if this all sounds a bit greek to you—you don't need to know this to play the songs in this book. Instead, these pages are intended for those who want to delve into the basics of reading music.

The staff

The **staff** is used to write down music. The staff is a group of five horizontal lines and the four spaces between them. It is read from left to right. At the end of the line you jump to the beginning of the next line. Notes can be written on the lines or the spaces in between.

Notes

There are different kind of notes, but they have one thing in common: Every note has a **notehead**. Most notes also have a **stem** and some of them an additional **flag** or a **beam**.

Pitch

Notes are written on the staff. You can tell the pitch of a note by its position on the staff. Notes from the third line on upwards have their stem pointing down. The stem of all other notes is pointing up. Notes that are too low or high for the staff are notated on **ledger lines**. You can think of ledger lines as a kind of abridged note lines.

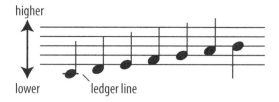

Note value

You can tell the note value (duration of the note) by its shape. The next smaller note  duration is derived by dividing the note value by two. For example: A half note is half the length of a whole note and two half notes once again add up to a whole note.

Rests

Rests are signs telling you to pause (e.g. play nothing) for a given period of time. For every note value, there's a corresponding rest. Don't mistake the whole rest for the half rest as they look quite similar!

Tip: Groups of eighth notes are usually notated using a beam—they're far easier to read this way.

Clef

The clef tells you the position of a reference note used to determine the positions of all other notes. If you see a G-clef, you can simply count: one note up from G = A; one note down from G = F and so on (see below).

This is an **F-clef**, telling you the position of the note F: the note F is located on the second line (counting from top to bottom).

This is a **G-clef**. It is the most common clef and tells you the position of the note G: the note G is located on the second line (counting from bottom to top).

Note names

There are seven different note names: A, B, C, D, E, F, G. After the seventh note, the note names repeat: A, B, C, D, E, F, G etc.

These seven notes are also called **natural notes** or **naturals**.

Below you can see one of the reasons there are several clefs: depending on the instrument, using another clef minimizes the number of ledger lines, making for a better readable notation.

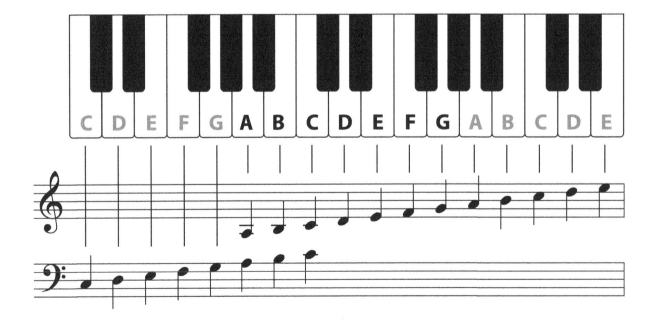

Accidentals

Take a look at the keyboard below. You'll see the note names you already know (white keys) but you'll also notice some new note names (the black keys). These new notes are created by raising or lowering one of the seven old notes.

♯ Writing a ♯ (sharp) before a note raises it by a half-step.
The note name is extended by an added "sharp" (e. g. G sharp).

♭ Writing a (flat) before a note lowers it by a half-step.
The note name is extended by the word "flat" (e.g. G flat).

Here are all the notes on a piano keyboard—memorize them carefully!

There are two ways to name the notes of the black keys. For instance, the black key between F and G can either be called F sharp or G flat. Don't let this confuse you—it's the same pitch nevertheless!

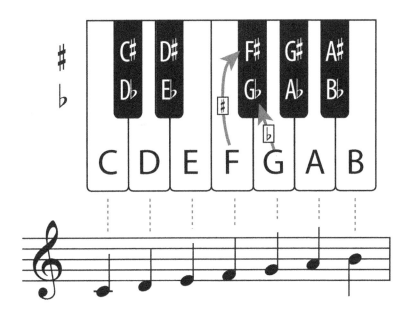

Key Signature

The **key signature** is a set of sharps (♯) or flats (♭) notated at the beginning of the staff immediately after the time signature. It designates notes that have to be played higher or lower than the corresponding natural notes. A sharp on a line or space raises all the notes on that line or space by a semitone. A flat on a line or space lowers all notes on that line or space by a semitone.

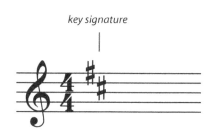

key signature

Bar (measure)

Notated music is divided into **bars** (or measures) by **bar lines**. The first note in every bar is accentuated slightly. The **time signature** at the beginning of the piece tells you how many notes make up a bar in this piece (here: 4 quarter notes). This time signature is called "Four-Four time". The end of a piece of music is indicated by a **final bar line**.

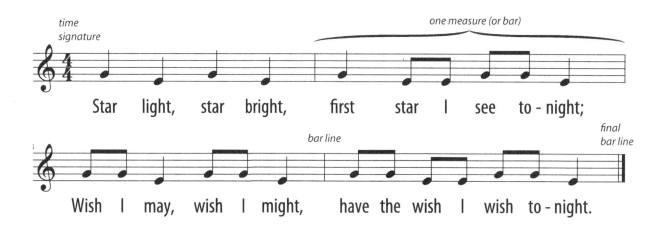

Time Signature

The time signature is notated at the beginning of the staff. It tells you how many beats each bar contains and which note value is equivalent to one beat. Here are some common time signatures and how to count them:

4/4 time

3/4 time

2/4 time

6/8 time

▲ = Stronger accent

▲ = Softer accent

Ties and slurs

Two notes of the same pitch can be connected by a curved line, the **tie**. The second note is not played separately. Instead, its duration is simply added to the duration of the first note (e.g. two tied quarter notes have the same duration as a half note).

There's another musical sign looking very similar to the tie, the **slur**.
Two or more notes connected by a slur are meant to be played independently, but seamlessly after another (also called legato playing).

The distinction between the tie and the slur is easy, however.
While the tie connects notes of the **same pitch and name**, the slur is only used on notes of **different pitches and names**.

Dotted notes

A dot behind a note increases the duration of that note by half its original length. This sounds much more complicated than it actually is:

A dotted half note has the duration of a half note plus a quarter note.

A dotted quarter note has the duration of a quarter note plus as eighth note.

Triplets

Dividing a note value by three instead of two is called a triplet. This sounds way more complicated than it actually is. Have a look at the graphic to the right. In standard notation, triplets are notated by the number "3" and often grouped with a small bracket.

A common way to count triplets is: "1-and-e, 2-and-e".

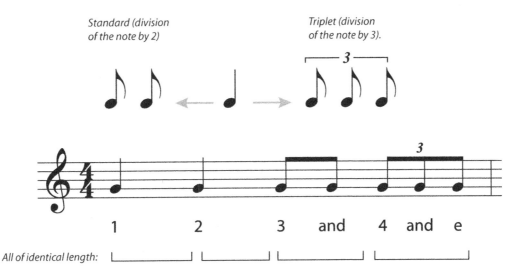

Repeat sings

These signs tell you to repeat parts of a piece of music (or even the whole piece).
Below are the most common:

This is the most basic repeat sign. It simply means: jump back to the beginning of the piece and play everything once again.

= 1 2 3 4 5 6 7 8 **1 2 3 4 5 6 7 8** (Repeated bars in bold letters).

Two repeat signs facing each other tell you to repeat everything between these signs once before continuing.

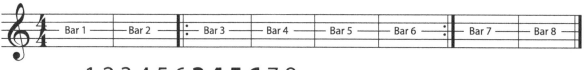

= 1 2 3 4 5 6 **3 4 5 6** 7 8

Numbered brackets above the music are used when a repeat calls for a different ending. These are called "first time bars", "second time bars" or first ending, second ending and so on.

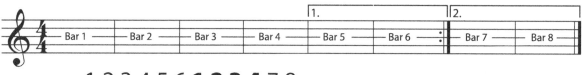

= 1 2 3 4 5 6 **1 2 3 4** 7 8

Another sign you're most likely to encounter is D.C. al fine (Da capo al fine).
It means: repeat from the beginning and play up to the word fine.

= 1 2 3 4 5 6 7 8 **1 2 3 4**

Dynamics

In music, "dynamics" means the variation in loudness between single notes, phrases or even longer sections of a piece of music. Traditionally, dynamics are notated in Italian.

These are the most common dynamic markings:

pp	=	pianissimo (very soft)
p	=	piano (soft)
mf	=	mezzoforte (medium loud)
f	=	forte (loud)
ff	=	fortissimo (very loud)

<	=	crescendo (gradually louder)
>	=	decrescendo (gradually softer)

Dynamics are always notated **below** the staff. Here's a short example:

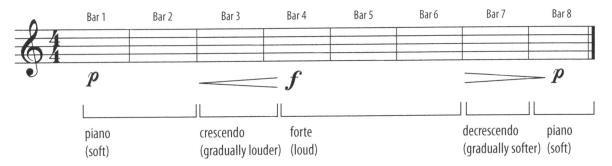

| Bar 1 | Bar 2 | Bar 3 | Bar 4 | Bar 5 | Bar 6 | Bar 7 | Bar 8 |

p   crescendo   *f*   decrescendo   *p*

piano (soft)   crescendo (gradually louder)   forte (loud)   decrescendo (gradually softer)   piano (soft)

To keep things simple, I didn't use dynamic markings in this book, but you'll encounter them sooner or later so the most important ones are included here.

In the unlikely case your tongue drum doesn't have printed tongue numbers, just cut out these templates and fit them to your drum with a piece of clear adhesive tape.

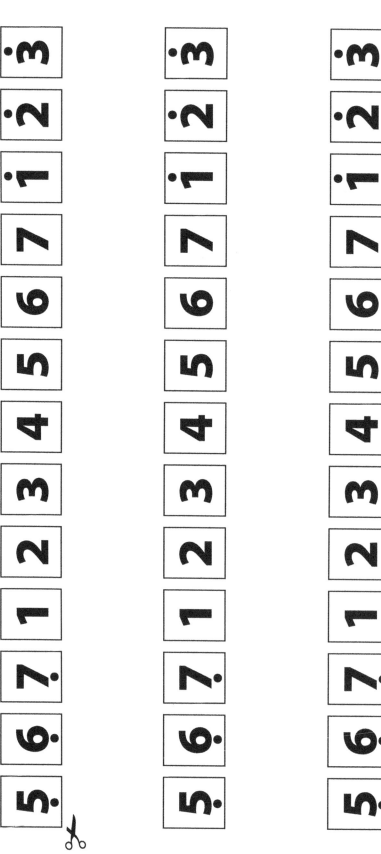

Made in United States
North Haven, CT
10 December 2024